IMAGES
of England

ROYAL
LEAMINGTON SPA

The parish church of All Saints is Warwickshire's largest church.

IMAGES
of England

ROYAL
LEAMINGTON SPA

Compiled by
Jacqueline Cameron

TEMPUS

First published 1999
Copyright © Jacqueline Cameron, 1999

Tempus Publishing Limited
The Mill, Brimscombe Port,
Stroud, Gloucestershire, GL5 2QG

ISBN 0 7524 1614 6

Typesetting and origination by
Tempus Publishing Limited
Printed in Great Britain by
Midway Clark Printing, Wiltshire

To Craig and Carol Bruce to mark the occasion of Craig's promotion.

The Leamington Spa coat of arms.

Contents

The marriage of David Lawrence and Angela Price on 24 April 1954 at Stoneleigh church. The bridesmaids were the bride's sisters Doreen, Josephine and Marion Price and Anne Lawrence, the sister of the groom.

Acknowledgements

The author acknowledges the help of the following people with thanks:

Graham Wilton, Dave and Angela Lawrence, Mr and Mrs Wagstaff, Jack and Molly Cox, Roz Crampton, Geoff Parker, Andrew Wild (senior and junior), Dave Wood, Pete Symonds, Georgina Halford, Terri Bayliss and the Records Office, Leamington Spa Library and Warwick Museum.

Introduction

Renowned for its Victorian painted stucco villas and beautiful Regency houses, much of the charm of nineteenth-century planning can still be found in and around the town of Royal Leamington Spa today. The River Leam, which divides the Old Town to the south of the river from the New Town to the north, played an important part in Leamington's history. To appreciate this, you have to go back to the days when Benjamin Satchwell the cobbler and his friend, William Abbotts the inn keeper, sort to bring prosperity to the town following the discovery of a second saline well on Abbotts' land. Interest arose after the discovery of the first well, several years earlier, which was known to have medicinal properties. Both Satchwell and Abbotts were anxious to exploit its potential.

The curative properties of the saline water brought about a change in the town's fortunes. From around 1770 all the signs were of a boom town with people visiting Leamington Spa to take the waters and new houses developed to cater for this sudden upsurge in popularity. This only lasted for a few years because, due to the cost of the war with France, there was very little progress in the town's growth between 1793 and 1806. Fortunately, this was only a temporary pause and between 1806 and 1820 new brick houses began to appear, with assembly rooms and hotels built to cater for the needs of the people. Bisset's Paragon Museum and the art gallery appeared and the town even had a fumigation bath called Fairweathers. All of this development was in the Old Town and it was not until 1810 that the town's Improvement Committee formulated plans for the land north of the River Leam; the fruits of which can still be seen today. Buildings with wrought-iron balconies and pediments, spacious terraces and crescents reflect the Regency trend of the time.

The Royal in the town's name originates from a visit on 3 August 1830 by Princess Victoria with her mother, the Duchess of Kent. In honour of the occasion, the town was allowed to add Royal to its name and this has remained a proud tradition ever since. Later in the 1830s, when Victoria had become Queen, she rested at the Regent Hotel on her way to Warwick Castle.

Leamington Spa, however, has more than saline waters and architecture in its history. It is difficult to associate this beautiful Victorian town with an abattoir, yet as late as 1939 there were no less than 18 licensed slaughterhouses between Holly Walk and Regent Street, where some 4,500 animals were slaughtered for human consumption. Horses also had a part to play in the history of the town because they were used long before transport became automated. Little boys could be seen walking after them carrying buckets and shovels in an effort to be environmentally friendly!

Another interesting piece of Leamington Spa's history is the aerodrome which could be found south-east of the village of Whitnash. It was small and uneven but conveniently situated to the south of the railway. Named after the village, it was to prove invaluable in the Second World War as it was so geographically well placed. Local industry was able to take advantage of the aerodrome for aircraft after it had been enlarged for the purpose.

In 1999 the town witnessed the opening of the refurbished Pump Room with the library and the art gallery, which have been in Avenue Road for many years, moving into this famous building. To appreciate the importance of such a move, you have to travel back to the days before free libraries when Messrs Bisset and Elliston served the Old Town with their library, and the Athenaeum, owned by Mr Bettinson, provided a similar service north of the river.

It was not until December 1855 that the first steps were taken towards establishing a free public library. The instigator was a well-known carriage builder called Henry Milliner who called a meeting of the town's people to discuss the idea. A committee was set up in January 1856 with impressive names such as Thomas Muddeman, John Silverside and Eve James sitting on the committee. In December of the same year the local board called a further public meeting to consider the adoption of the Free Libraries Act. When it was put to the vote, ninety-four people were in favour and twenty were against. The necessary room was found in the Town Hall on the High Street to keep the 1,000 books that were purchased and Mr Saunders became the first librarian. The building was opened on 16 March 1857 and statistics show that the attendance figures on the first day were four people in the morning, ten at midday and sixty in the evening. There was also a free reading room in the town which was available for the public, thanks to the generosity of Captain Dunscombe, a man who took great interest in the working classes of the day. The reading room was situated in Covent Garden and, although Captain Dunscombe appealed to the authorities for a more central position, his request was turned down and he eventually presented his books to the Free Library.

By November 1858, when the library moved to its own premises on the corner of Church Walk, there were 1,050 books, though 500 of these were classed as unreadable due to the fact that they were publications of the commission of patents. Thanks to the introduction of a lending library, which was opened on 8 September 1859, an extra 1,000 books were purchased. A ladies' reading room was added in April 1863. The Free Library was to move many times in its history but, thanks to the enthusiasm of Dr Thursfield, a most enthusiastic worker for the library, a building in Avenue Road was built. The building cost £16,000 and the foundation stone was laid by the Mayor Alderman J.M. Holesworth. The architect was Mr J. Mitchell Bottomley of Leeds and Middlesborough, the builder a Mr Richard Bowen of Tavistock Street, Leamington Spa, and the opening ceremony took place on 12 December 1902.

For some time the lack of a suitable gallery to exhibit pictures which had been presented to the town and for displaying other collections had been a problem. In 1927 the decision was made to build a cruciform art gallery as an annexe to the library. The council decided to pay half the cost and in May the following year the foundation stone was laid by Lord Elgin. The work continued throughout the year and the art gallery was opened by Sir Charles Holmes in early December. It is interesting to observe that during the Second World War the art gallery was requisitioned by the Government for use by the Camouflage Division.

Now, thanks to the refurbishment of the Pump Room, scheduled for re-opening in June 1999, the library and art gallery will be housed in the same building.

One
A Town of Character

The oak tree, or 'Round Tree' as it has been known for centuries, is said to mark the centre of England and was thought to be one of the old Gospel Oaks. Standing alongside Cubbington Road, it finally succumbed to old age and was felled in 1960. It has been replaced by a sapling.

The Desmond, a private first-class hotel with forty-two bedrooms, stands on the corner of Kenilworth Road and Clarendon Avenue. The proprietress was Mrs Gower in the early 1930s.

The Leamington and Warwick Tramway was three miles long and ran from the Avenue Station in Leamington Spa to the High Street, Warwick.

Looking up the Parade from the Victoria Bridge. The bridge can be found in the New Town area of Leamington Spa.

On the left of this late 1920s view of the Upper Parade is Bedford Stores. From 1874 it was known as Burgis and Colbourne after two of the town's tradesmen amalgamated their businesses and opened a shop in Bedford Street in an effort to stop trade that was going to London. The venture proved such a huge success that they extended their Bedford Street premises to the Parade. The business went on to trade in Leamington for many years.

Trinity Chapel, Beauchamp Square. The date in the bottom right-hand corner reads March 25th 1851.

The War Memorial in Leamington Spa can be found at Euston Place. The long list of those who perished can be seen around the base.

The Regent Hotel opened in Leamington Spa on 18 August 1819 and was the brainchild of Mr and Mrs John Williams. Sadly, the building closed in January 1999 and awaits redevelopment.

This picturesque view of the Victoria Bridge shows a punter on the River Leam. The building on the right is the Washington Hotel and the parish church is prominent in the centre. The Happy Christmas message at the top suggests that it was one of a number of cards used to promote the town.

The Royal Pump Room and Bath is currently undergoing redevelopment and is scheduled for completion in June 1999.

The elegant Victorian Town Hall and the Bright Obelisk, which was erected in 1880 in honour of Alderman Henry Bright.

Newbold Terrace is a beautiful Regency setting with fine houses that have single- and two-storey porches. Until as late as 1839, only two or three houses at each end of the terrace had been built.

Catholic Church, Leamington Spa.

Designed by Mr H. Clutton of New Burlington Street, London, and built by Mr G. Gascoyne of Newbold Terrace, St Peter's church stands in Dormer Place. It was opened on 18 August and the tower was added in 1877.

The Jephson Gardens lake is one of the focal points in the gardens. It attracts many visitors, such as those seen here feeding goldfish.

Originally known as Union Row, the Parade, as it is now known, is one of the most scenic views in the Victorian town of Leamington Spa.

Holly Walk got its name from the holly trees that flourished from Newbold Comyn, the home of the Willes family, to the Parade. Sadly, there are only a few holly trees found there now and these can be seen in Upper Holly Walk.

This view shows Linden Avenue at its most tranquil. The large glass globe in the centre of the archway is a gas light, which was lit by somebody who acted as a gas lighter.

Victoria Terrace is one of Leamington's oldest. Seen here around 1908, it can still be found in the Old Town.

A pair of young children peer cautiously over the edge of Victoria Bridge. The Pump Rooms, which were reconstructed in 1999, can be seen in the background.

One of the most impressive buildings in Leamington Spa is the parish church of All Saints. It is seen here looking from the Victoria Bridge towards Old Town.

Charles Crowden moved from Bath to 10 Eastnor Grove, Leamington Spa, in 1898. At his motor works in Packington Place he produced the only type of car produced in Leamington, the Crowden Light Car. Unfortunately it never went into serious production, although Mr Crowden remained in the town until 1904, when it is believed he retired. An example of the car can be seen in the Museum of British Transport in Coventry. The car in the picture was owned by Mr M.J. Carpenter until around 1930, when it was sold. Sitting in the car is Mr Carpenter's youngest daughter.

The Parade, Parish Church and Pump Room, Leamington Spa.

On the right are the Pump Rooms. In the early days they were the only means of bathing for the poor of the town who could not afford their own bathroom. For a shilling, which included a slipper bath and towel, they could bathe and have the bath cleaned up after them. A tram can also be seen travelling down the Parade and the parish church stands in the background.

This statue of Queen Victoria can be found standing proudly in front of the Town Hall.

The Aylesford Well was situated outside All Saints parish church. It has now been demolished and replaced by a plaque.

The garden and summer house of the Desmond Hotel.

The Congregational church in Spencer Street. The building is no longer a church but is used as a carpet sales room.

The impressive building in the centre of this photograph of Dormer Place was the National Tailoring Company who ran a very upmarket tailor's shop. After the tailors' business ceased, the premises became a branch of the National Westminster Bank before being converted to its present use as a restaurant.

This view of the Parade and the Victorian Town Hall was taken around 1905.

The parish church of All Saints was originally a chapel belonging to Leek Wootton. The architecture dates from the twelfth century, though the church was partially restored in 1624.

The famous Monkey Walk, with the tranquillity of the Parade on a sunny afternoon in leafy Leamington. Unfortunately, over a period the trees have been thinned a lot since this picture was taken.

Victoria Terrace, looking very much as it does today, although the awnings and the trams would no longer be seen.

LEAMINGTON, BOATING LAKE.

The boating lake, with the rustic bridge which leads off to the Mill Gardens, in 1911.

River Walk, Leamington Spa.

The beautiful river walk of Leamington Spa. In the distance the Adelaide Road Bridge and the tower of St Peter's Catholic church can be seen. The circular flower beds no longer exist.

A delightful view of the Jephson Gardens. The ladies in the centre of the picture take a pause while walking their dog.

The peaceful River Leam, in contrast to spring 1998 when it flooded badly. In the background is an early view of the Pump Rooms.

The Jephson Gardens have two fountains that are replicas of those found at Hampton Court. The original fountain was installed in 1925 and an identical one was installed at the other end in 1926. Both fountains have underwater floodlights, thanks to the generosity of Alderman A. Holt who donated money towards the cost.

ROYAL PUMP ROOM GARDENS, LEAMINGTON SPA.   2/3278

The Pump Room gardens in the 1920s. St Peter's church is in the background with its pineapple steeple (origin unknown). A fire that started in the organ brought about the steeple's demise later in the 1920s.

This tranquil picture of the Mill Gardens was taken around 1900.

The 1999 facelift of the Pump Rooms will undoubtedly change them a great deal. This is a reminder of how they used to look.

One of the stylish dining rooms at the Desmond Hotel that captures the 1920s beautifully.

St Michael's and All Angels church, which was later renamed St Alban's, had its foundation stone laid on 7 June 1877. After leaving his Christchurch congregation in 1881, Dr Nicholson purchased St Michael's for £5,600 a year later. On 1 January 1903 the tower was erected to commemorate Queen Victoria's Jubilee. The original chapel became a fully independent parish church in 1903.

Euston Place gardens in 1988 with the famous Pump Rooms in the distance.

The Pump Rooms and the Parade. The tramlines stretching into the distance and the weather tower on the Pump Rooms are clearly visible.

This unusual sketch of the Town Hall makes a refreshing change from the usual photographs of the town. The Bright Obelisk can be seen on the right and was erected in 1880 in front of the main tower.

The large building in the centre of this aerial view of Newbold Terrace was the headquarters of the Free Czech Forces who were stationed in Leamington Spa during the Second World War. Two from the forces, Jan Kubis and Joseph Gabcik, accomplished their mission when they parachuted into Czechoslovakia in 1942 and executed General Heydrich, the chief of the Gestapo. As a reprisal, the Nazis exterminated the villages of Lidice and Lezaky. Sadly, Jan Kubis and Joseph Gabcik lost their lives.

Taken in 1932, this photograph shows the effects the swollen River Leam had on the town when it flooded the Pump Rooms and Jephson Gardens.

Harrington House, the large building on the right, is prominent in this aerial view of Leamington Spa. The town's Spa Centre now stands on the site where Harrington House used to be.

The new River Walk stretches three-quarters of a mile from Adelaide Bridge to the railway arches. The arches span the River Leam by Princes Drive.

S 17107   The Clock Tower, Leamington Spa

The Davis Clock Tower was dedicated to Alderman W. Davis by his wife in May 1926. It is situated near the Newbold Terrace entrance to Jephson Gardens. The clock was silenced because of the amount of noise from its Westminster Chimes in the 1930s, but restored in memory of Mrs Joy Beeby in 1986.

This view of the bandstand in the Pump Room gardens shows how different it looks today. The trees have been thinned out, the bushes no longer exist and the bandstand has hanging baskets in the summer. In the late 1930s the railings were melted down as part of Leamington's war efforts.

LEAMINGTON, PUMP ROOM GARDENS.

These young ladies are out for a walk in the Pump Room gardens during the early 1900s. Each one is wearing a fashionable gown and hat.

This 1912 scene shows the view looking down Brunswick Street in the Old Town. The young boy in the foreground would have been unable to pose like this today!

The Hitchman Fountain was built in 1869 as a memorial to Dr Hitchman who was a believer in hydropathic treatment. He was also responsible for erecting an arboretum in the town.

The bandstand, which can be seen in the Pump Room gardens to this day, is the venue for local brass bands. In the summer months and on special occasions when the town celebrates its history, people come to enjoy the gardens and the music.

One of the many photographs of the York Walk Promenade, taken early this century. Its tranquillity contrasts with the hustle and bustle of the previous picture. The flower beds that graced the river bank unfortunately no longer exist. The message at the bottom of this postcard reads, 'Many happy returns of the day from Sam and Mag.' The writing and the postmarks (which are dated 1904) on the reverse suggest that it has been to Paris and back via Southam.

The Free Library was built in 1902. The Leamington Municipal school was part of the library building in Avenue Road.

The trees on the famous Linden Avenue were planted in 1928.

Victoria Bridge, which was first built in 1808, was much smaller in design than its replacement, built in 1840. The bridge was enlarged again in 1848. The impressive building which can be seen in the background is the general Post Office.

This unusual postcard shows the moon shining over the Pump Rooms. In the distance the parish church can be seen.

The windmill on Tachbrook Road. The sails were removed in 1943 and the building was eventually demolished in 1986.

The elegant Clarendon Avenue West. The large house on the corner with Beauchamp Square was the home and business premises of Edgar Ringer the horse vet.

Linden Walk was more commonly known as the Monkey Walk. The glass globe in the centre of the picture was lit by a gas lighter each day. From here, the poor in the community would watch their more affluent counterparts take afternoon tea in the Pump Room gardens.

The Leamington Spa Church of England Sunday school demonstration was obviously a popular event. This one took place on 13 May 1923.

This entrance to the beautiful Jephson Gardens shows the lodges that were designed by Mr D. Squirhill and erected in May 1846. A stipulation was made that the lodges were not to exceed 30ft from the ground to the ridge of the roof. Hence their low appearance.

An early photograph of the Jephson Garden lake. The most obvious features missing are the fountains and the ducks.

An early photograph of the Lillington church. Between 1066 and 1291 Lillington was recorded as a separate parish.

Boating on the River Leam at the turn of the century. In the background Willes Road Bridge can be seen.

Shrubland Hall was the home of Matthew Wise, one of the three most influential people in Leamington Spa's history. This beautiful house was built in 1823 and until this date Matthew Wise had lived at the Manor House, which is now a hotel in Avenue Road. Two and a half storeys high, Shrubland Hall had a small beech lawn and a Victorian lodge at the eastern end of the house's drive. On the death of Charles Wise, Matthew's son, the house became a private school for girls, until 1939. Its demise came shortly before the Second World War when the Shrubland Estate was developed. The Victorian lodge ended its days as a builder's office.

An aerial view of the Town Hall and the Parade to the north of the River Leam. The Bright Obelisk can clearly be seen in the centre of the picture.

An aerial view of the Mill Weir and the suspension bridge that was opened in June 1903. Based on the Albert Bridge, London, it joins the Jephson Gardens and the Mill Gardens.

Situated in George Street, the Boys Mission Hall began its days as the first Roman Catholic church. Built to the design of Russell and Mitchell, architects from Wise Street, it was opened by the Rt Revd Dr Walsh on 1 October 1828. The chapel was dedicated to St Peter and cost £1,000 to construct.

This walled garden could be found at the Desmond Hotel.

THE HOLLY WALK, LEAMINGTON.

The Holly Walk ran from Newbold Comyn to the Parade and down to London Road, which is now the present High Street. The building on the right is the Regent Cinema that sadly no longer exists and in the distance the Town Hall clock tower can be seen.

The Pump Room gardens had railings that skirted the river bank in the middle of the 1800s.

This view of the York Walk was taken from Adelaide Road.

These delightful figures began their days on the opposite side of the Parade but can now be found in Euston Place above an estate agents.

Looking down the Parade in the 1950s with Thomas Logan's premises on the right and Woodward's the drapers in the centre.

On the right of Bath Street the former Temperance Hotel and the Coffee Tavern could be seen.

THE ROYAL PUMP ROOM & BATHS, LEAMINGTON.

The Royal Pump Room and Baths. Note the weather tower and a gas light as they looked around the turn of the century.

Two
A Peep into the Past

LEAMINGTON SPA

Great Western Railway employees in their final group picture. Some of these men were seen with armbands in the Local Defence Volunteer days.

The lady on the right is Mrs Ena Burton. She is seen here with her mother who lived to be over 100 years old.

Lil Shepherd and her older brother enjoy each others company in the garden, late 1920s.

George and Bessie Cox posed for this photograph with their son Tom at the front gate of their house.

Lillian Cox enjoys a few precious moments in the back garden with her nephew.

The Avenue Bowling Club in 1955.

The Lillington Snooker Club men's 'A' team. Back row, left to right: -?-, Jim McCarthy, Peter Holloway, Harry Ramage. Front row: John Purvis, George Prick, Dave Lawrence, Stan Richards and Arthur Ellis.

Mr and Mrs Samuel Cox celebrate their
Golden Wedding Anniversary.

Mrs Shepherd and her daughter Lillian in
the late 1920s.

Mr Joseph Lawrence was a gamekeeper.

George Ivens was in the RAF and Marge Ivens was a policewoman when this photograph was taken during the Second World War.

Girls involved in munitions work during the First World War.

Lucy Hemmings (left) and a friend posed for this picture on the balcony at the Pump Rooms where they worked as waitresses.

The children of Radford Semele and their parents pose for a group photograph at the annual Maypole celebrations in 1926. This event was run every year by Mr Hemmings.

Alec Payne and his son Barry on McGregors Field, Pound Lane, Lillington, in 1929.

The 1934 Campion school hockey team. Back row, second right is Beryl Lawton. In the middle of the front row is Pauline Yates and extreme right is Betty Payne.

Lillington Sunday school was run for many years by Mrs Smallwood and her daughter. Those involved in this production from the 1930s include Jean Ham, Connie Owen, Janet Wickes, Ms Mills, Betty Wagstaff, Rosemary Fennell, Betty Wickes and Nancy Greenway.

St Paul's scout group, c. 1939.

This picture of the Hemming family was taken at Radford Semele in 1921.

The Lillington Pound Lane keep-fit class in 1949. In the back row are Ann Baldwin and Betty Wagstaff, and in the centre of the front row is the dance teacher.

The staff at Shrubland Hall, around the turn of the century.

In the centre of this smartly dressed group is Lucy Hemmings at Shrubland Hall in 1899.

In Loving Remembrance of
DEAR WILL,

The beloved Son of EDWARD and ANNIE HERRINGSHAW, of Leamington,

Aged 23 Years,

Translated to Glory by a Lightning Flash, after preaching at Marton,

On Sunday, Feb. 20th, 1910,

On the Subject of: "From Death to Life."

JOHN v, 24.

He was ready, are you?

Copies may be obtained of F. Quaintance, Printer, Leamington.

Lay preacher Will Harringshaw met his demise in 1910 when he was just twenty-three years old. The story goes that he was on his way home from preaching at Radford Semele church when a bolt of lightning struck him while he sheltered under a tree.

The Lillington football team, around 1917. Among the players were brothers Walter and Alec Payne.

On the left, Barry Payne and his sister Betty play in the hay on the Campion Hills in 1929. The cornfields that were in Lillington are much talked about and this picture provides evidence of their existence.

A Lillington dancing class, around 1950. The little girl in the centre of the front row is Linda Wagstaff.

In 1935 the Wagstaff's family car was a BSA three-wheeler with four cylinders.

Lillington school in 1930. Front row, left to right: Jean Ham, Iris Bradley, Ethel Halloway, -?-, ? Reed, Jean Pittaway. Second row, second right is Peggy ? and extreme right is Irene Batty. The third row includes Nancy Greenway, Rosy Fennell and Janet Wickes, the fourth row Connie Owen and the back row Betty Payne.

Joan and Roy Bentick stand on the steps of the Spencer Street Congregational church after their wedding in the 1960s.

Alec Kord poses in front of the flowers at Jephson Gardens in the 1940s.

Jacqueline and Gillian Cox posed for this photograph in 1948.

Bill Wilson holds a white handkerchief for some of the blind and partially sighted bowlers of Leamington Spa in the 1970s.

On the back of this postcard reads, 'Father says he has just come and it don't matter where he sleeps'.

This picture of a mother and her children illustrates some of the typical fashions worn in the late 1800s.

Three
All in a Days Work

Mr Dick Barnes' retirement presentation in 1965. Those present from left to right are: Tru Hayford, Ron Lovett, Dick Barnes and Mick Morrisey.

Once a year the local mayor and civil dignitaries visited the Ford Motor Company. Here we see one of the guests trying his hand at pouring metal on the number one mould line, watched by the Plant Manager, George Jackson (wearing glasses), in the early 1960s.

Workers' Playtime was a popular radio programme that took place during the Second World War and for a period afterwards. Performances in works' canteens were given during the dinner hour by artists and musicians brought in to entertain the employees and then broadcast live.

Sir Anthony Eden MP (left) goes through the working of a Fordson tractor ploughing attachment. Anthony Eden was the Conservative MP in Leamington Spa for many years after the Second World War.

MAIN FORD DEALERS

C.H.SOANS & SON, LTD

F. C. SOANS M.I.M.I. MANAGING DIRECTOR

AUTOMOBILE ENGINEERS

528

DORMER PLACE
OPPOSITE REGAL CINEMA

LEAMINGTON SPA
TELEPHONE 2206 (2 LINES)

DATE
Sept 1957

W.Wicks Esq.,
Flat 3. 43 Buckley Road,
Lillington . Leamington Spa

Sept	14	J.184					
		2. Indicators	E62A.118002		2	5	0
		1. Switch				12	6
		5. Pints Castrolite				8	7
		2. Pints Gear oil				4	8
		Popular 987 EEV.					
		5,000 miles service and lubrication as per hand					
		book. Tighten all shock absorber and body bolts.					
		Fit flush fitting trafficators and wire up.			5	0	0
					8	10	9

17534

DORMER PLACE, LEAMINGTON.

4 - 11 - 1957

Rec'd of

M. W.Wicks Esq

the sum of £ 8 :10 :9

For

C. H. SOANS & SON,
Ltd.

WITH THANKS.

STRICTLY NETT MONTHLY

A C.H. Soans & Son invoice for W. Wicks of 43 Buckley Road, Lillington. C.H. Soans & Son had premises for their automobile engineering business at Dormer Place.

Ernie Thornley's farewell
presentation from his work
colleagues at the Imperial Foundry
in the 1960s. Those also present
included George Jackson the Plant
Manager, Tony Worrall, Roly
Wood, Cis Mullard, Dave Chase,
Bob Partridge, Walter Cobb, Ernie
Webb.

One of Leamington's much loved
characters was Rene Randall who
devoted her life to the town and for
a period was the mayor. She is seen
here taking a tour of the Imperial
Foundry with Ron Lovett who had
succeeded George Jackson as the
Plant Manager in the 1960s. After
Ron Lovett came Don Rutherford,
Ron Bowdidge and Bruce Bell, the
present Plant Manager.

Plant Controller Phil Davidson worked for eighteen years at the Ford Motor Company in Princes Drive from December 1974 until 1993.

Miss Bishop supervised the typing pool at Lockheed for many years before her retirement. She was famous for ruling with a rod of iron.

The Flowers and Son Brewery dray, photographed in Leamington Spa, where the company had a depot. The steam driven lorry, the metal wheels and the barrels of beer all convey the 'feel' of the old days.

The Flowers Brewery dray leaves the depot in the late 1930s. The Poachers sign on the side of the wagon was a familiar sight.

Another Workers' Playtime during the Second World War.

Members of the Ford Motor Company receive the Gold Safety Award. From left to right: Steve Whitby, -?-, Bruce Bell (Plant Manager), Jack Cox (Safety Officer), Jimmy Dunne.

The Imperial Foundry scrapyard in the early 1950s. The Grafton crane on the left of the picture loaded the scrap metal into skips or containers which were then transported by Jubilee Gauge Railway to the cupolas (melting apparatus). The scrap pile would be transported by a combination of road and rail.

The press shop at Sidney Flavel's in the 1920s. Though called the Eagle Foundry, it was known locally as Flavel's Foundry. The foundry was responsible for the manufacture of cookers, coal and basket grates and their famous fireplaces.

Flavel's Foundry in the 1920s.

The staff of Flavel's Foundry, Princes Drive, around the turn of the century.

A group of children receive gardening lessons outside Wolverton school.

The annual office party at the Imperial Foundry in the 1960s. Those visible in the picture include Mrs Gladys Hill, Bob Jones, Bill Jones, Colin Haywood and Dave Wood.

Brian Knibb (left), Bill Jones and Ron Williams, who worked together at the foundry's laboratory, enjoy a joke together.

Kathleen Woodward (back) instructs her pupil, Annette McCarthy, on the art of flower arranging at the local college.

A Conservative victory in one of the General Elections in the 1970s. From left to right: -?-, Jenny Buckworth, Terri Bayliss, Dudley Smith MP, his wife Catherine and Gladys Cleeland.

Taken in 1934, this early photograph of Lockheed Automotive Products automotive block shows several horses and carts waiting for instruction while the building was under construction.

The workers at Lockheed Automotive Products during the Second World War.

The Queen Mother meets the catering staff at Lockheed Automotive Products during a visit on 6 November 1958.

Perhaps one of the most successful businesses in Leamington Spa is A.C. Lloyd. Established in Camberwell Terrace in 1946, the founder was Mr Cyril Lloyd, a carpenter and joiner. The business has won numerous awards for building and design skills over the years.

Another Workers' Playtime, this one in 1944, at the Imperial Foundry. The Imps' concert party includes Mrs Brown, Mr Williams, Mr Bob Hood, Mr Smallwood, Mr Fox, Miss Cooper, Don Austin, Mr Cape and Mr Murphy.

Putting the cope onto the drag at the Imperial Foundry. The man on the right is Dave Flowers.

Staff at the Ford Motor Company after receiving awards from the Plant Manager, Don Rutherford. Back row, left to right: Sid Sleeman, Mr Jones, -?-, Mr Reagan, -?-, Mr Grant, -?-, Mr Gardner. Front row: Eileen D'Arcy, Don Rutherford, -?-.

Ron Bowdidge the Plant Manager hands over the keys of the minibus donated by the Ford Motor Company to the Leamington Boys Club.

Four

At Play

The Lillington Snooker Club men's 'A' team in the mid-1950s. Back row, left to right: Stan Rickards, George Price, John Purvis. Front row: Reg Cotton, Ken Waite, Dave Lawrence, Harry Ramage, Peter Holloway.

These young men and women took part in a Lockheed pantomime in the 1940s. Performances like this were well supported at the time because there fewer distractions, like television. Those present include Lt A. Lawrence, Lt Clay Thomas, Capt. Payne, Sgt Major Reg Aston, Daisy Ashcroft, Rosalie Fennel, Doris Adams, Jose Fennel, Iris Ward and Rita Paulton.

In the 1960s, Christmas parties for employees' children were an annual event and would include stage shows and a visit by Father Christmas. These happy, expectant faces at the Imperial Foundry say it all.

Three Ford golf players tot up their scores on the Campion Hills.

A dinner at the Regent Hotel, c. 1947. Front row, left to right: -?-, Mrs Inman, Harold Inman. Second row: -?-, -?-, Brab Parham and his wife, Mrs and Mr Gardner. 'Ray' Rayment is on the third row and those along the wall include George Jackson, Mr Roly Wood and Sammy Barriscale.

Daisy Humphries (right) must be one of Leamington Spa's most dedicated fund-raisers. She is seen here collecting used birthday cards for the Helen Ley M.S. home from the author.

This is a meeting of friends in the 1980s. Those present include Jo Williams, John Everitt, Jackie Kord, Keith Robbins, Liz Bullas, Mrs E. Bateman, Kath Green, her husband Norman Green and Pat Green.

Dave Lawrence shows off his Triumph motorbike in the 1930s.

The Ralph Callaway quiz took place in 1973 at the Guy Nelson Hall, Warwick school. From left to right: John Everitt, Sid Foster, Glyn Morgan, Dave Sanders.

Arthur Shurvington and Bill Lawrence stand in front of one of the local buses.

The winners of the annual Potterton/Ford Friendly Cup for bowls. From left to right: Pete Creffield (senior), George Bubb, Colin Haywood, Bill Port.

It's a Knock Out took place on the Edmondscote sports track in 1971. Back row, left to right: Graham Gardner, Les Justice, -?-, -?-, Sid Foster, -?-, Trevor Bingham, Phil Stanley, -?-, -?-, Tom Jennings. Front row: Hadyn ?, Miss Green, Pat Manley, -?-, Miss Toone, Eileen Ross, Phil McKeown.

Campion high school football club senior team in 1963.

Ford's cricket team in 1950. Back row, left to right: Bill Higgins, Tommy Streeter, -?-, -?-, Dick Bowmer, Charlie Stratton, Cis Manley, Ken Cheshire. Front row: -?-, -?-, Frank Herbert, Tony Hoffman (senior), -?-, Tommy Buchan.

A Workers' Playtime at Lockheed in the 1940s.

Two little boys pull a Christmas cracker at the Imperial Foundry children's Christmas party in the early 1950s.

This sack race took place at the Ford Motor Company Sports and Social Club ground in Myton Road, in the early 1970s.

This Signs of the Zodiac entry was one of the floats taking part in the popular Leamington Carnival in the middle of the 1960s.

Some of the blind bowlers of Leamington in action.

Sue Probert (back) and Annette McCarthy demonstrate flower arranging for a Leamington flower club in the early 1980s.

Leamington Avenue Bowling Club.

One of the bell-ringers at Cubbington church.

The entrance to the Town Hall, when it was being decorated to celebrate Randolf Turpin winning the world middleweight title against Sugar Ray Robinson in 1951. The gentleman on the left is George Ivens. The van belongs to Sims' electrical shop which still has branches in Warwick and Leamington Spa.

Lillington Snooker Club men's team. From left to right: Pete Hiley, John Purvis, John Grimster, Dave Lawrence. Front row: John Prentice and Alex ?.

Leicester Street Central School for Girls' nativity play in 1936.

Five
Around the Area

The High Street, Kenilworth, in the late 1880s.

The picture for this postcard of Kenilworth Castle was taken from the south side.

Leicester's Buildings, Kenilworth Castle. The castle is still imposing despite the damage it has suffered.

Ashow Church, from River Avon.

This tranquil scene of Ashow church was taken from the River Avon.

OLD COTTAGES, ASHOW.

A row of old cottages at Ashow.

These two views of Leek Wootton were taken in the late 1800s. Known as 'the Saxon town in the wood', to its east is the neighbouring hamlet of Hill Wootton. The village has a late eighteenth-century church which has a fifteenth-century tower.

Piers Gavestons Monument can be found near Leek Wootton in the Warwick direction on Blacklow Hill. Brought up in Edward I's royal household as a foster brother to the king's eldest son (Edward II), Piers Gaveston was made the Earl of Cornwall in 1307. A proud and greedy man who made many enemies, he was captured by the Earl of Warwick and taken to Warwick Castle where he was sentenced to death. The monument in the picture marks the spot where Gaveston had his head struck off on 19 June 1312. His body was taken to Oxford by Dominican monks where it remained for two years before being buried in King's Langley, Hertfordshire, on 2 January 1315.

The River Avon, near Warwick Castle. The gentleman standing on the steps, behind the boat, is Samuel Bissell.

Guy's Cliffe Avenue near Warwick.

Standing on a steep slope overlooking the River Avon is the ruin of Guy's Cliffe House. The legendary Guy of Warwick is reputed to have retired to live here and given the house its name. It is known that hermits occupied a cave situated nearby which became the property of St Sepulchre's priory. The house was passed on to the Percy family in 1826 and they lived there until 1946 when it was sold. Sadly, the roof caved in 1996 and the building has been left to ruin.

Hatton church near Warwick. The church has a very fine lych-gate which, unfortunately, is not visible in this view.

Leigh House, Hatton Asylum, is now being developed into a prestigious housing estate.

The Hampton-on-the-Hill Football Club team from the 1921-22 season. Front row, left to right: E. Tracy, T. Collett, G. Bourton, B. Vincent, T. Field. The players on the middle and back rows are not known.

The Durham Ox public house at Shrewley Common.

The Old Red Horse pub stood in Norton Lindsey for many years. Unfortunately, the building was demolished to make way for a housing complex in 1970.

Wolverton primary school. The man with the hat, and beard, is the headmaster, Mr Smith.

This building has stood the test of time and can still be found at Wolverton Fields where it is still used as a school. This photograph was taken in the mid-1920s when Mr Smith was the headmaster.

Four young children pose for this photograph in Wolverton.

The smithy at Aston Cantlow.

The Square, Snitterfield. The New Inn public house is the first building on the right.

Pratts the tailor and the Swan Hotel are on the right-hand side of this street, thought to be in Southam.

The post office (left) at Wilmcote.

Mr Sammy Lane stands outside Mary Arden's house in Wilmcote.

This picture of Alveston was taken around 1910 at the wash near Tiddington.

Children feature in this picture of Carters Lane, Tiddington, around 1917.

The church at Hampton Lucy can be seen on the right, although the picture is dominated by the trees in the centre.

This look around Barford features Bridge Street, the mill, St Peter's church, Wellesbourne Road and Church Street.

Buildings along School Road, Wellesbourne, *c.* 1953. The old black and white building was a farmhouse, the building on the right was probably a tied cottage for the workers on the farm and the cottage on the left was privately owned. The doctor's surgery now stands on this piece of waste ground.

The Agricultural College at Moreton Hall. The spectacular piece of statuary attracts the attention of a group of visitors.

The picturesque village of Combroke can be found three or four miles south of Wellesbourne.

Mr and Mrs Steve Mumford stand in the doorway of their public house, the Royal Oak, in Whatcote.

A picturesque view of the Fosse Way near Kineton.

This look around the village of Kineton features Southam Street, Banbury Road, Bridge Street, St Peter's church and Warwick Road.

This desolate looking view of Bishops Tachbrook, far removed from how it looks today. The area seen here was transformed into the Tachbrook housing estate in the early part of the twentieth century.

The date 1688 can be seen on the front of Western House in Harbury.

This delightful cottage was in Ladbrooke.

Shakespeare's birthday celebrations, Stratford-upon-Avon, in 1939. The Southam Hairdresser can be seen in the background, but why is the Nazi swastika flying from the flagpole?

Coventry Street, Southam.

Abbey Green, Southam. Close by Abbey Green is the Abbey House, which had associations with the priory in Coventry. In the garden are some very old, protected yew trees.

The famous Southam well.

Radford Semele village, around the turn of the century.